EGYPT

WORLD ADVENTURES

BY STEFFI CAVELL-CLARKE

KidHaven
PUBLISHING

Published in 2018 by
KidHaven Publishing, an Imprint of Greenhaven Publishing, LLC
353 3rd Avenue
Suite 255
New York, NY 10010

Designer: Matt Rumbelow
Author: Steffi Cavell-Clarke

Cataloging-in-Publication Data

Names: Cavell-Clarke, Steffi.
Title: Egypt / Steffi Cavell-Clarke.
Description: New York : KidHaven Publishing, 2018. | Series: World adventures | Includes glossary and index.
Identifiers: ISBN 9781534524019 (pbk.) | 9781534523999 (library bound) | ISBN 9781534525191 (6 pack) |
ISBN 9781534524002 (ebook)
Subjects: LCSH: Egypt–Juvenile literature.
Classification: LCC DT49.C38 2018 | DDC 962–dc23

Printed in the United States of America

CPSIA compliance information: Batch #CW18KL: For further information contact Greenhaven Publishing LLC, New York, New York at 1-844-317-7404.

Please visit our website, www.greenhavenpublishing.com. For a free color catalog of all our
high-quality books, call toll free 1-844-317-7404 or fax 1-844-317-7405.

EGYPT
WORLD ADVENTURES

CONTENTS

Page 4   Where Is Egypt?
Page 6   Weather and Landscape
Page 8   Clothing
Page 10   Religion
Page 12   Food
Page 14   At School
Page 16   At Home
Page 18   Families
Page 20   Sports
Page 22   Fun Facts
Page 24   Glossary and Index

Words in **bold** can be found in the glossary on page 24.

WHERE IS EGYPT?

Egypt is a country located in northern Africa. The capital city of Egypt is called Cairo.

EGYPT

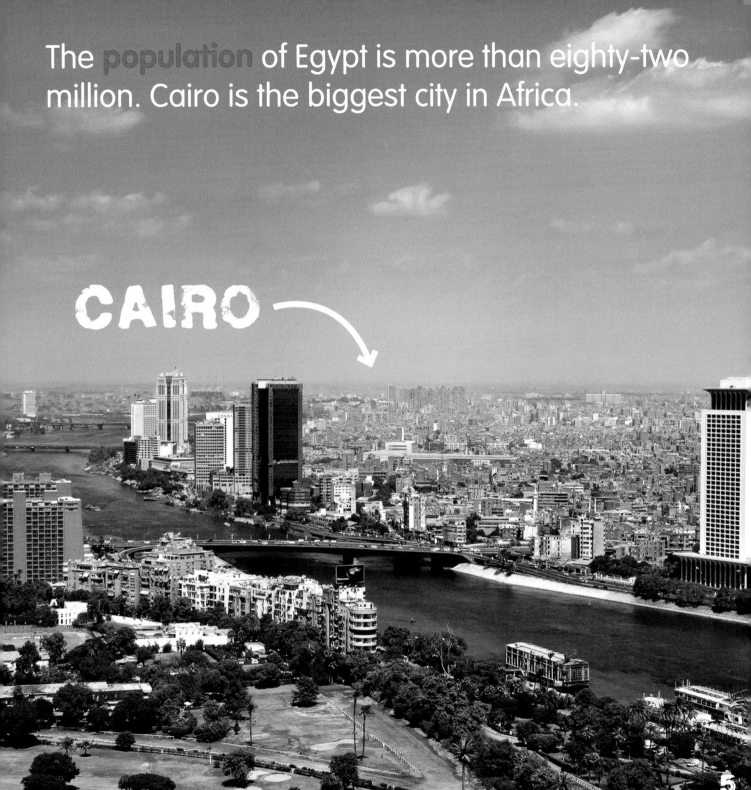

The population of Egypt is more than eighty-two million. Cairo is the biggest city in Africa.

CAIRO

WEATHER AND LANDSCAPE

Most of Egypt is sandy desert with a hot and dry climate. It has very hot summers and mild winters.

PYRAMIDS IN GIZA

Nearly everyone lives near the Nile River. They use the river for water, food, and **transportation**.

The Nile is the longest river in the world.

CLOTHING

TAQIYAH
(HAT)

Egyptian men usually like to wear loose clothes to keep cool. They also like to wear cloth hats to protect their heads from the sun.

Many Egyptian women wear long dresses and headscarves. This headscarf is called a hijab.

HIJAB

RELIGION

The religion most followed in Egypt is Islam. People who follow Islam are called Muslims. Their place of **worship** is called a mosque.

THE MOSQUE OF MUHAMMAD ALI IN CAIRO

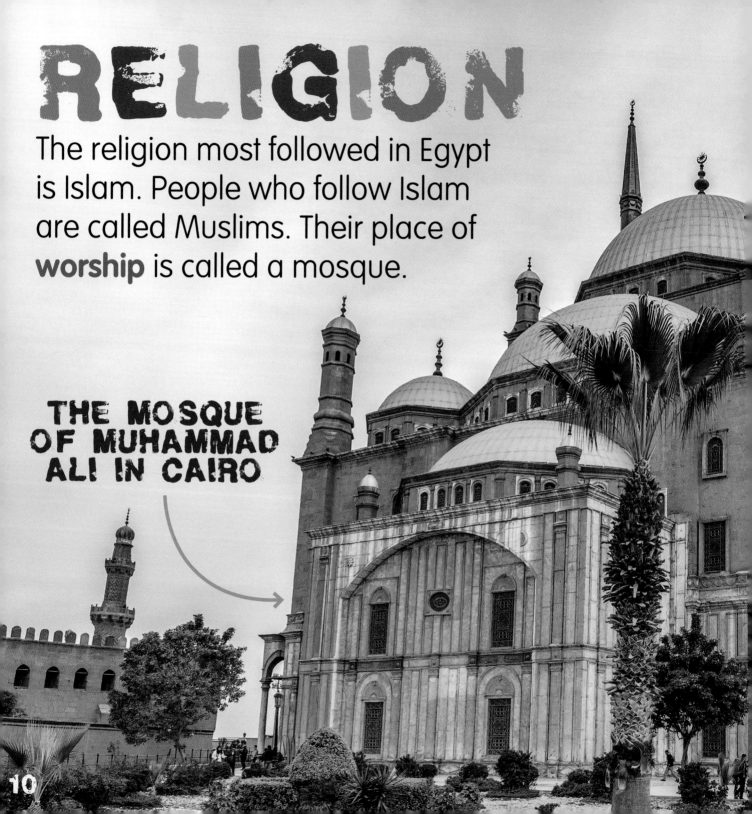

Men, women, and children must wash their hands and feet with clean water before they enter the mosque as a sign of respect to God. This practice is called Wudu.

Shoes must be taken off before entering a mosque.

FOOD

Egyptians mainly eat wheat bread, rice, and vegetables that are grown in the large fields next to the Nile. Sometimes they eat fresh fish from the Nile and the Red Sea.

COOKED FISH FROM THE NILE

An Egyptian meal often starts with lots of small healthy dishes, such as falafel and hummus. They are both made from chickpeas.

FALAFEL

HUMMUS

CHICKPEAS

13

AT SCHOOL

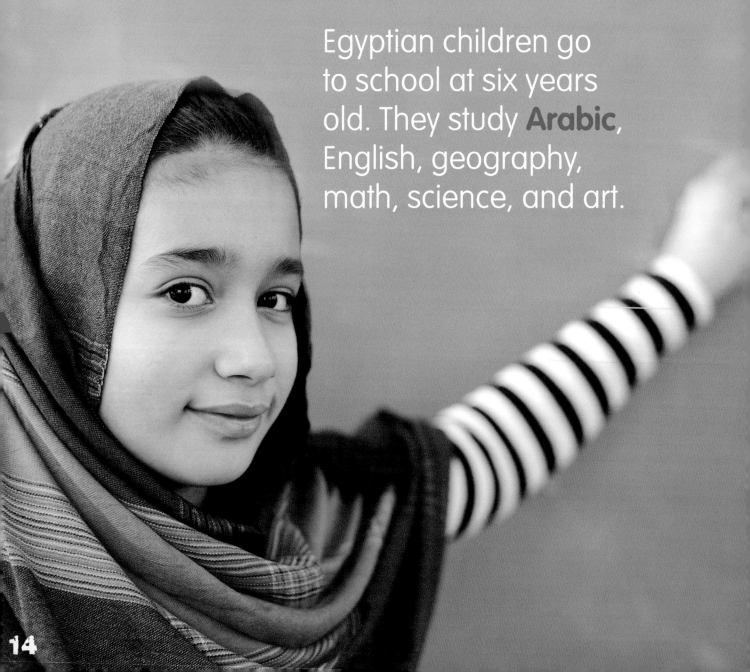

Egyptian children go to school at six years old. They study **Arabic**, English, geography, math, science, and art.

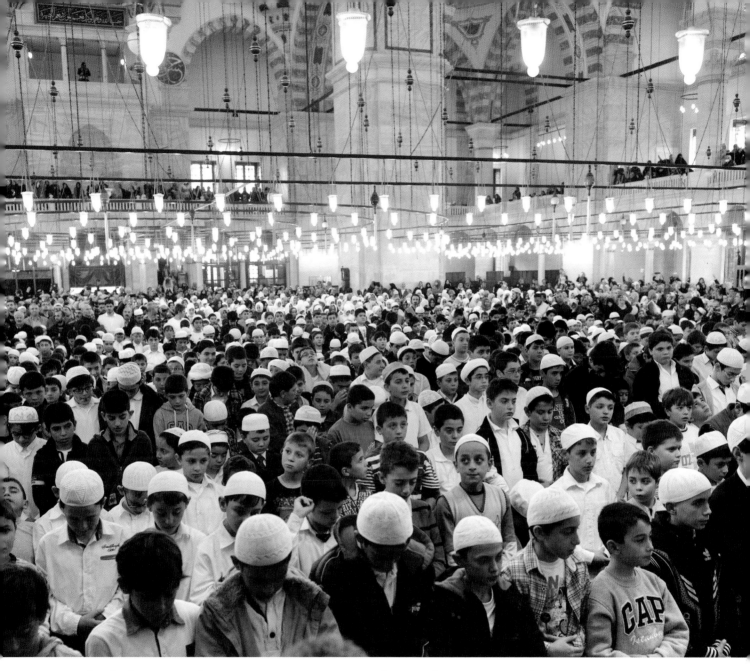

Children do not go to school on Fridays as it is a Muslim holy day. Instead, they often visit the mosque for prayer.

Egyptian families can be very large and they often live together.

Some families live on large farms in huts made of mud bricks. Others live in apartments in the cities.

APARTMENTS IN CAIRO

FAMILIES

Women usually stay at home to look after the children while the men go to work.

Families get together for special **occasions** such as birthdays and weddings.

SPORTS

Soccer is the **national** sport in Egypt. Lots of children like to play soccer after school with their friends.

Egyptian children also like to play basketball, handball, and tennis.

FUN FACTS

There are over one hundred pyramids in Egypt.

PYRAMIDS WERE BUILT THOUSANDS OF YEARS AGO, AND STILL STAND TODAY.

Egypt is home to a large number of animals including camels, crocodiles, and dung beetles.

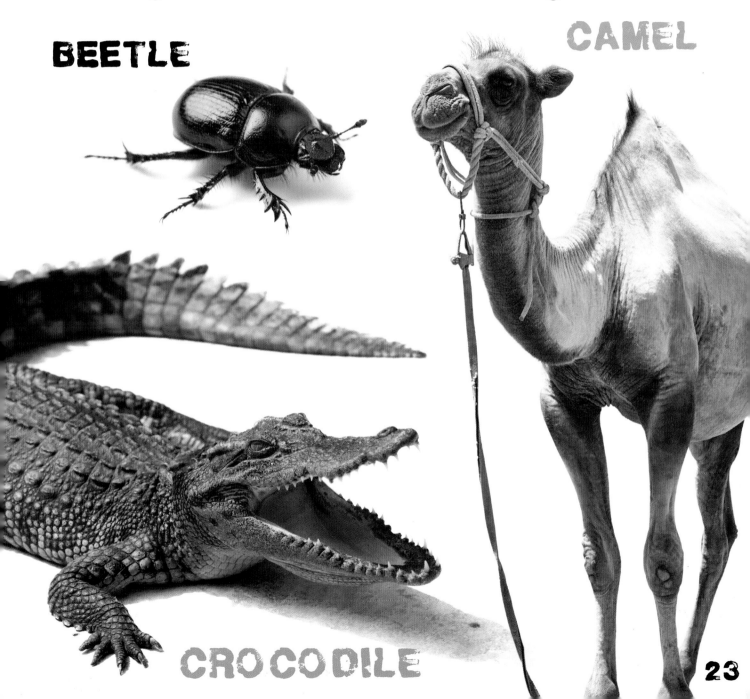

BEETLE

CAMEL

CROCODILE

GLOSSARY

Arabic: a common language spoken in North Africa and the Middle East

climate: the weather in a large area

national: common to a country

occasions: special events to celebrate

population: amount of people living in that place

transportation: a way of getting from one place to another

worship: a religious act, such as praying

INDEX

camel: 23

cities: 4, 5, 10, 17

family: 16, 17, 18, 19

food: 12, 13

mosque: 10, 11, 15

Nile: 5, 7, 12

pyramid: 6, 22

religion: 8, 9, 10, 11, 15

school: 14, 15, 20